DRESSING A NATION
THE HISTORY OF U.S. FASHION

CALICO
DRESSES
and BUFFALO
ROBES

American
West
FASHIONS
from the
1840s
to the
1890s

KATHERINE KROHN

TWENTY-FIRST CENTURY BOOKS
MINNEAPOLIS

Dedication

To a great editor and friend, Margaret Q. Goldstein

Front cover image: This photograph from the late 1800s shows a woman dressed in a calico dress with ruffled shoulders and collar. The simple dress and hairstyle were common for women living in parts of the American West in the 1800s.

Back cover image: A Plains Indian wears a buffalo robe, as well as moccasins and leggings. He also has a bow and arrows strapped around his shoulders.

Page 3 image: This American woman wears a calico dress and has her hair pulled-back in a typical style of the late 1800s. She has a lace handkerchief tucked into the top pocket of her dress.

Twenty-First Century Books
A division of Lerner Publishing Group, Inc.
241 First Avenue North
Minneapolis, MN 55401 U.S.A.

Website address: www.lernerbooks.com

Library of Congress Cataloging-in-Publication Data

Krohn, Katherine E.
    Calico dresses and buffalo robes: American West fashions from the 1840s to the 1890s / by Katherine Krohn.
        p.   cm. — (Dressing a nation: the history of U.S. fashion)
    Includes bibliographical references and index.
    ISBN 978-0-7613-5890-9 (lib. bdg. : alk. paper)
        1. Clothing and dress—West (U.S.)—History—19th century—
2. Fashion—West (U.S.)—History—19th century—Juvenile litera
(U.S.)—History—19th century—Juvenile literature. 4. Men's cloth
19th century—Juvenile literature. 5. Indians of North America—
literature. 6. Frontier and pioneer life—West (U.S.)—Juvenile lite
and customs—19th century—Juvenile literature. I. Title.
GT617.W47K76 2012
391.00978—dc22
                                                                         2011003036

Manufactured in the United States of America
1 – DP – 7/15/11

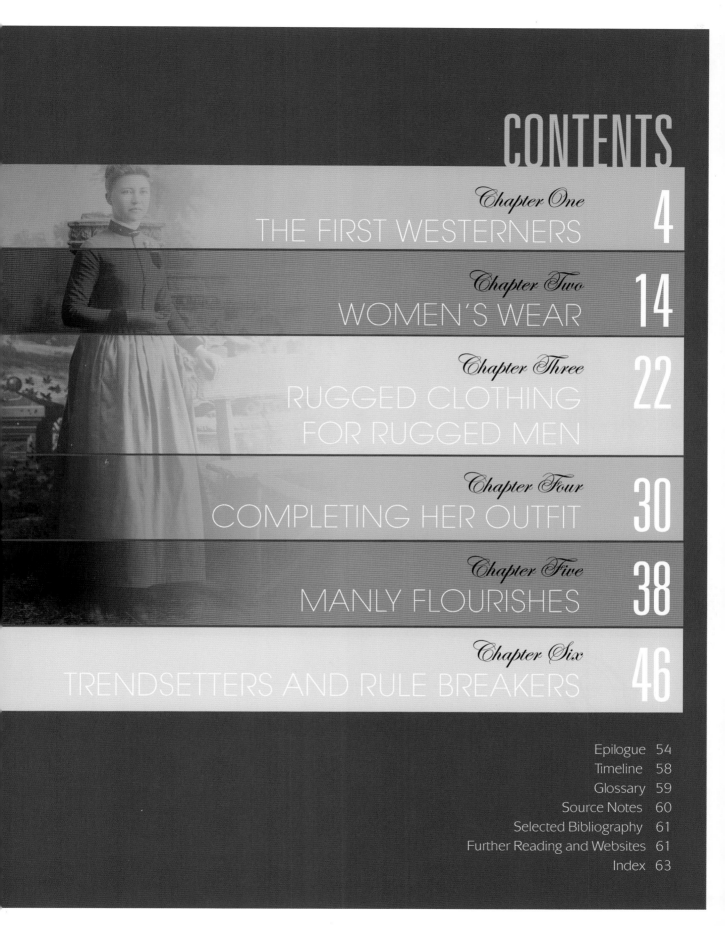

CONTENTS

Chapter One

THE FIRST
WESTERNERS

These westward-bound pioneers take a break in Colorado in the 1800s. Pioneer women on the trail wore practical printed dresses and aprons. Children sometimes went barefoot, while men wore boots, sturdy trousers, and a plain shirt. On the trail, most travelers wore the same outfits over and over again.

On April 24, 1849, a young woman named Catherine Haun set out with her husband from a town in Iowa to the goldfields of California. They traveled with a group of about twenty-five others, each family with its own wagon. The journey took the travelers across the Great Plains (lying between the Mississippi River and the Rocky Mountains), the Rocky Mountains, and western deserts. In a trunk in her wagon, Catherine had packed two blue-checkered dresses, as well as undergarments, aprons, and colorful bonnets. But she didn't wear any of that clothing on her journey west. Instead, she wore a plain woolen dress. On her head, she wore a simple cotton kerchief.

Like most western travelers, the Hauns walked next to their wagon for much of the overland journey. Catherine, her husband, and their fellow travelers encountered dust, mud, thorns, and thick brush as they walked. The sturdy fabric of Catherine's woolen dress protected her skin from these hazards. The dress also kept her warm on cold days. Water was in short supply, especially in the desert. Washing clothes regularly was not an option. So Catherine kept wearing the same woolen dress, even when it was dirty.

The Hauns arrived in Sacramento, California, in November, six months after starting out. In Sacramento, they joined thousands of others who had come west hoping to find gold. These California gold seekers were only one portion of a vast flood of settlers who moved to the American West in the middle and late 1800s. Farmers, businesspeople, writers, entertainers, and laborers of all stripes came west in search of land, fortune, and sometimes fame. Most of these newcomers came from the eastern or midwestern United States. Most were white people of European descent.

Historians called the years 1837 to 1901 the Victorian age, named for Britain's Queen Victoria. Victorian-era fashions were quite elaborate, featuring lots of frill and flounces. London, England, and Paris, France, were fashion hot spots during this era. Especially in the eastern United States, Americans took their fashion cues from these cities.

But for American westerners of the Victorian era, high fashion was not a top priority. Keeping warm, dry, and safe was their main concern. Farmers, trappers, miners, and other western laborers needed clothing that was durable—not necessarily stylish or good looking. Like Catherine Haun, they needed clothing that would stand up to the hazards of life in the rugged West.

The styles that Britain's Queen Victoria wore in the mid 1800s were the height of fashion. She is shown in this 1854 photo wearing an ornate gown, embroidered with flowers and edged with lace. Queen Victoria's fashion style influenced American women's fashion. In the United States, including the American West, many women copied her style for parties and special occasions.

INDIANS ARRIVED FIRST

The overland travelers who came west in the 1800s were not the first western inhabitants. Native Americans, or Indians, already called the West home. Each Indian tribe had a unique culture and distinct traditions. The clothing that each group wore depended upon the climate, the terrain, and the natural resources available.

Until Europeans arrived in the Americas, Native Americans made all their own clothing by hand. They used these raw materials:

- **animal hides**
- **animal furs**
- **plant fibers**

Men usually hunted and butchered the animals. Women used stone scrapers to clean the hides of animal hair and flesh. They treated the hides with chemicals from the brains of deer. The chemicals turned the hides into leather, which doesn't decay the way untreated hide does. Women softened the leather with animal fats and then sewed it into garments. They made sewing needles out of stone or animal bone. They used animal sinew (cord made from tendons) or plant fibers as thread.

PLAINS TRIBES

The American Great Plains were home to dozens of Native tribes in the 1800s. These Indians included the Crow, the Mandan, the Sioux, the Cheyenne, the Ponca, the Pawnee, the Arapaho, the Kiowa, and the Osage. These groups made most of their clothing from skins from deer and buffalo.

This Crow Indian man wears a breechcloth in a photo taken around 1900. Some Native Americans wore very little clothing, especially in warm weather.

A Plains Indian man might wear a little or a lot of clothing, depending on the weather and the time of year. At the very least, he wore a breechcloth to cover his groin and backside. This garment consisted of a long piece of deerskin. The wearer wrapped it between his legs and secured it with a band around his waist. He left two long flaps hanging down— one in front and one in back. Plains Indian men wore deerskin leggings, shirts, and ponchos for extra warmth and protection from the elements. Plains women wore loose-fitting deerskin skirts and dresses. In cold weather, they also wore ponchos, leggings beneath their dresses, and other extra layers.

This Pawnee woman wears a buffalo robe in this photo from 1868.

Both Plains women and men wore buffalo robes in winter. Buffalo fur is extremely warm. Plains people also wore rabbit fur shawls and vests. On their feet, they wore deerskin moccasins.

Plains Indians often decorated their clothing. They adorned dresses, shirts, leggings, and other garments with these:

- **leather fringe**
- **bird feathers**
- **beads**
- **paint**
- **bird and porcupine quills**

For special ceremonies, men wore headdresses made of skins of deer and buffalo. They decorated the headgear with feathers, dyed horsehair, and beads. Some Plains Indians made earrings out of copper, shells, and animal bones.

THE MYTH OF THE FEATHERED HEADDRESS

In modern times, when people think of Native American clothing, they sometimes imagine an Indian man wearing a big feathered headdress (such as the one a Cheyenne man is wearing in the 1878 photo at right). This image is a stereotype. It comes from TV shows, movies, and advertisements of the early and mid 1900s. In reality, only a few tribes of the Great Plains wore feathered headdresses. These headdresses were warbonnets. Warriors wore them in battle and for special ceremonies. The bonnets were made of eagle feathers, with each feather symbolizing an act of honor or bravery.

GREAT BASIN PEOPLES

West of the Plains, across the Rocky Mountains, sits the Great Basin. This vast desert territory was home to a number of western tribes, including the Ute, the Bannock, the Shoshone, the Paiute, and the Washoe. Great Basin peoples used the skins of deer and rabbit to make clothing. They also used bark and other plant fibers. They stripped bark from trees and shredded the soft inner fibers into narrow strands. Women wove the strands together to make fabric.

In summer, Great Basin peoples did not wear much clothing. Men wore breechcloths. Women wore skirts made of woven sage bark. People often went barefoot, but they sometimes wore sandals made of these:

- **deerskin**
- **rabbit skin**
- **yucca fibers**

In winter they braided strips of rabbit fur to make warm robes.

This photo from 1883 shows a woman of the Shoshone tribe. She wears a hide dress decorated with beads. Her moccasins also have beading.

INDIANS OF THE
Columbia Plateau

North of the Great Basin is the Columbia Plateau, the region surrounding the Columbia River. The Indians of this area include the Klickitat, Yakama, Umatilla, Cayuse, Nez Percé, Coeur d'Alene, and Flathead. Plateau Indians wore clothing made from the skins of rabbits and deer. Garments included these:

- **close-fitting pants**
- **leggings**
- **shirts**
- **dresses**
- **moccasins**

Plateau Indians also used plant fibers to make clothing. Women made skirts out of bark cloth and hats out of dried leaves, grasses, and other plant materials. Both men and women wore rabbit fur and elk skin robes to keep warm. In the western plateau, people often went barefoot. To the east, they wore deerskin moccasins. Like the Plains peoples, Plateau Indians often decorated their clothing with paint, fringe, and beading.

"**THEIR USUAL** DRESS WAS A FROCK AND LEGGINGS AND MOCCASINS **MADE FROM** DRESSED DEER SKIN, AND A WELL DRESSED **BUFFALO SKIN... FOR A BLANKET,** TO RIDE ON AND SLEEP IN."

—JOHN BALL, WHITE EXPLORER AND FUR TRADER DESCRIBING THE FLATHEAD INDIANS OF IDAHO, 1832

Left: A Nez Perce man wears a striped blanket coat, beaded leggings, and moccasins. He is also wearing beads in his hair and around his neck. Many Indians of the Columbia Plateau (in what is now the state of Washington) made clothing and other items (such as the bag at right) from plant fibers.

Coastal Peoples

Dozens of Indian tribes lived along the northwestern coast of the Pacific Ocean, in the modern-day states of Washington and Oregon. These groups included the Tlingit, the Haida, the Nootka, the Kwakiutl, the Squamish, the Skagit, and the Chinook. Like other Native American peoples, they used animal skins, furs, tree bark, and plant fibers to make clothing. They used the wool of mountain goats to make warm blankets. Since they lived along the seacoast, they also used materials from sea animals. For instance, they created warm, water-resistant robes from the fur of sea otters. Men of the northwestern coast sometimes went naked but sometimes wore full-length tunics made of woven plant fibers. Women wore skirts and capes, also made from plant fibers. To keep their heads dry in this rainy region, some people wore round or cone-shaped hats. These too were made from woven plant fibers.

For ceremonies, some groups wore carved wooden masks and headdresses, painted in bright colors. Northwest coast people made jewelry out of animal bone and shells. Many groups tattooed their faces and bodies. The tattoos represented their clans, or family groups. The pigments, or colors, came from minerals and plants.

Farther south along the Pacific coast lived the California Indians. Peoples of this nation include the Shasta, the Pomo, the Salinas, the Chumash, and the Cahuilla. Some California tribes, particularly those on the southern coast, enjoyed a warm climate much of the year, so they wore little clothing. Men often went naked or wore only skin or bark breechcloths. Women wore skin, grass, or bark skirts. People sometimes wore ankle-high deerskin moccasins or sandals made from yucca fibers. They used plant fibers to make hats. When it did get cold, people used sea otter fur, bird feathers, and rabbit skin to make robes and blankets. Women often adorned their skirts with fringe and beads. Both men and women wore earrings made of these:

- **animal bone**
- **seashells**
- **beads**

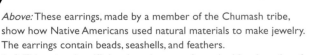

Above: These earrings, made by a member of the Chumash tribe, show how Native Americans used natural materials to make jewelry. The earrings contain beads, seashells, and feathers.
Left: This painted wolf's head mask comes from the Nootka tribe of the Pacific Northwest. A tribe member would have worn this mask for special ceremonies.

INDIANS OF THE
SOUTHWEST

The American Southwest is home to the Hopi, the Navajo, the Apache, the Pueblo, and other Native American peoples. These groups also made clothing out of animal skins, fur, bark, and other plant fibers. The Pueblo people grew cotton and spun it into cloth. Like other Native Americans, Indians of the Southwest made these:

- **breechcloths**
- **dresses**
- **shirts**
- **ponchos**
- **boots**
- **moccasins**
- **sandals**

They decorated their clothing with paint, fringe, and beadwork. For ceremonies, the Hopi people wore elaborate masks adorned with corn husks, feathers, and other natural materials.

This young Hopi girl was photographed in the late 1800s wearing a cotton dress and shawl. The Hopi grew cotton and used its fibers for making fabric for clothing. She wears her hair in the squash blossom style, made by wrapping the hair around two wooden forms.

MIXING TRADITIONS

The Indians of North America often traded with neighboring peoples. In this way, clothing traditions spread from tribe to tribe. For instance, people in the Great Basin wore buffalo robes acquired from Plains Indians. People in the Southwest acquired seashells from coastal tribes in California.

When Europeans explored the Americas, starting in the late 1400s, they introduced new animals and materials to the Indians. For instance, Spanish settlers brought sheep to the American Southwest in the late 1500s. So the Navajo people began to raise sheep. They used sheep's wool to make clothing and blankets. Traditionally, Native Americans made beads out of animal bone, stone, and seashells. White traders later brought colorful glass, ceramic, and metal beads to the Indians. Native craftspeople incorporated the new beads into their traditional designs. In some cases, white westerners adopted some clothing traditions from the Indians. Many white trappers, fur traders, and explorers began wearing these:

- **deerskin pants and shirts**
- **buffalo robes**
- **moccasins**

In this photograph from 1883, most of the clothing—such as robes, footwear, and jewelry—is unique to the Crow people. But one woman wears a checkered cloth shirt or dress—a European American style. She might have gotten the garment on a reservation, where the U.S. government supplied clothing.

At the same time, some Indians added ready-made clothing—acquired from white traders—to their traditional outfits.

CHANGING CLOTHES

The arrival of Europeans greatly impacted the lives and cultural traditions of Native Americans. Europeans wanted to settle North America from coast to coast. They wanted Indian land and used a variety of tactics to acquire that land. After the creation of the United States in the late 1700s, the takeover of Indian land became an official part of U.S. policy. The U.S. government designated parcels of land to be Indian reservations. In many places, soldiers rounded up whole tribes and marched them to far-off reservations.

On reservations, U.S. government agents pressured Native Americans to assimilate (blend) into the white, European-based culture of the United States. Agents discouraged traditional Indian religion, language, clothing, and other cultural customs. Removed from their homelands and hunting grounds, Native Americans could not carry on their traditional livelihood. Instead of hunting animals for food and clothing, they began to rely on government-supplied food. They also wore ready-made, government-issued clothing—cloth dresses for women; and trousers and shirts for men.

SCHOOL *Uniforms*

In the late 1870s, the U.S. government took the assimilation of Indians into white society one step further. It required some Native American children to attend government- or church-run boarding schools, far from their home reservations. In some cases, the authorities arrested and imprisoned parents who refused to send their children to boarding school.

At the boarding schools, Native American children were forced to abandon their traditions completely. They had to speak only English and were punished for using their traditional languages. Teachers assigned each child a European American name to replace his or her Indian name. Teachers also dressed children in uniforms that were modeled on styles worn by European Americans of the era.

Traditionally, both male and female Indians wore their hair long. At boarding schools, however, staff cut boys' hair short. They cut and styled girls' hair to follow European American hair styles. Eight-year-old Gertrude Simmons, from the Dakota tribe, remembered having her long hair cut when she entered White's Manual Labor Institute in Indiana. She said, "I cried aloud, shaking my head all the while until I felt the cold blades of scissors against my neck."

At boarding schools, Native American students were required to wear their hair in short European styles. They were also forced to wear European clothing, as shown in this photo of students at the Carlisle Indian Industrial School in Pennsylvania in the late 1800s.

This young woman works in the field near her homestead in Colorado. She wears a traditional sunbonnet, calico dress, and sturdy leather lace-up boots. Many women in the American West dressed for the hard work they did all day on the farm.

Chapter Two

WOMEN'S WEAR

Most western women worked from sunup to sundown and into the late hours of the night. Their work included caring for children, cooking, baking, cleaning house, and washing clothes—and without any modern conveniences such as running water or electric stoves. Besides doing housework, many women farmed. They helped their husbands break ground on new homesteads and tend the fields.

For a typical day of housework and farmwork, a western woman usually wore a floor-length dress with a full, gathered skirt and a fitted bodice (the upper part of the dress). Dresses were made from these fabrics:

- COTTON
- *linen*
- MUSLIN
- WOOL

NINETEENTH-CENTURY
FABRIC GUIDE

brilliantine: a fabric made from a mix of fibers (typically including wool, mohair, cotton, and silk) with a shiny finish; often used to make dresses, linings, and dusters (long, loose coats)

broadcloth: a lustrous wool or cotton fabric

brocade: a heavy silk fabric with raised gold or silver designs

calico: a cotton fabric, often decorated with tiny floral patterns

cambric: a soft linen or cotton fabric; often used to make handkerchiefs, pocket linings, underwear, and shirts

canvas: a coarse, durable cotton or linen fabric

denim: a tough, cotton fabric originating in France

felt: a nonwoven fabric made from wool, fur, or animal hair. Felt makers use heat, moisture, and pressure to lock the fibers together into a tight mat.

flannel: a soft cotton or light woolen fabric with a slight nap (raised fibers)

gingham: a woven cotton cloth with a checked pattern; often used to make dresses

linen: a fabric woven from fibers of the flax plant

linsey-woolsey: a fabric made of linen and wool

mohair: a fabric made from the long, strong hair of the Angora goat; often used to make warm items such as sweaters, winter suits, jackets, and scarves

satin: a woven fabric with a shiny front and a dull back; originally made from silk

serge: a strong woolen cloth

silk: a soft, shimmery fabric made from the cocoons of silkworms

Calico, a heavy cotton—usually decorated with a floral pattern—was the most popular fabric for everyday dresses. Linsey-woolsey, a combination of linen and wool, was also common. Women sometimes called the cloth wincey, because it scratched their skin and made them wince.

Farm women wore long aprons, which protected their dresses from dirt, snags, and tears. Aprons tied in the back and usually had pockets for carrying small objects.

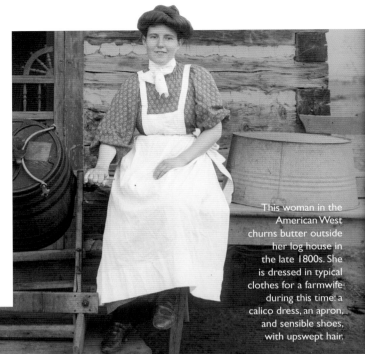

This woman in the American West churns butter outside her log house in the late 1800s. She is dressed in typical clothes for a farmwife during this time: a calico dress, an apron, and sensible shoes, with upswept hair.

Sunday Best

A few wealthy western women owned a wardrobe full of luxury items, such as silk and satin dresses, embroidered shawls, expensive jewelry, and silk stockings. If a woman had the money, she could hire a seamstress to make a special, custom-fitted dress for her. City women, especially in port cities such as San Francisco, had access to styles and fabrics from far-off places. For instance, Luzena Stanley Wilson was able to purchase "genuine finery," including crepe shawls and scarves, delivered by "Chinese vessels which came into San Francisco."

But for most western women, fine garments were rarities. People wore fine clothing only on special occasions, such as at weddings, funerals, church services, and dances. Etta May Lacey Crowder grew up in Iowa in the late 1800s. She noted that most pioneer women couldn't be bothered with ruffles, lace, and beading. As she later wrote in her memoirs, "At that time a clean calico dress was plenty good enough for church or Sunday school and a gingham or calico sunbonnet frequently took the place of a hat."

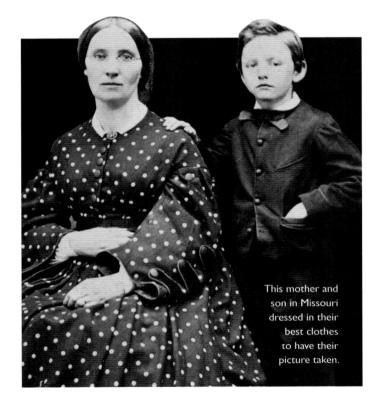

This mother and son in Missouri dressed in their best clothes to have their picture taken.

MAKING DO

In the West, people often lived miles from the nearest town or trading post. When garments wore out, it wasn't easy to get new ones. So westerners made do with the resources at hand.

Some farm families owned sheep and made warm clothing out of sheep's wool. With spinning wheels and other tools, women turned raw wool into yarn. Florence Courtney Melton's family moved from the Midwest to Oregon in the 1860s. In the spring, Florence helped her mother sheer sheep, wash the raw wool, and prepare it for spinning. "Then Mother's work began in earnest," Florence said. "She had it all to spin and color [dye], to send to the weaver."

"**EVERYTHING** WE TRAVEL THROUGH IS THORNY AND ROUGH. **THERE IS NO CHANCE** TO SAVE YOUR CLOTHES."

—ELIZABETH SMITH, TRAVELER ON THE OREGON TRAIL, 1845

Westerners who owned sheep could make warm clothing out of wool. These women in Minnesota gather to card, or comb, wool fibers in preparation for making them into yarn.

Other farmers grew a plant called flax. They spun flax fibers into linen thread. Some farmers grew cotton, which they spun into cotton thread. After spinning, farm women used hand looms to weave strands of yarn or thread into fabric. Then they cut and sewed the material to make simple garments—work dresses for women and girls, and sturdy work pants and shirts for men and boys. Some white women learned from their Native American neighbors. They used deerskin, buffalo hide, and rabbit fur to make shoes, moccasins, coats, and blankets.

Considering how hard it was to make or acquire new clothing, it made sense for westerners to wear the same clothes again and again. Families also handed down clothing items from one child to the next. If an item of clothing ripped, a mother or a daughter mended it. If the clothing was beyond repair, she packed away any usable scraps of fabric to patch other clothing or to make a quilt. She also cut off the buttons and saved them for later use. Some western families even made clothing out of old grain or sugar sacks.

Top: A woman mends clothes in this painting by artist Wilhelm Hasemann from the late 1800s. Women in the 1800s spent a lot of time making clothes. They mended them so they could be worn for a long time.
Bottom: This family was photographed on their homestead in Nebraska in 1887. Their clothes were probably homemade and were typical of farm family clothes at the time—sturdy shirts and pants for men and dresses with aprons for women.

LITTLE WOMEN

Girls on the frontier typically dressed like their mothers. They wore ankle- or calf-length dresses made of cotton or linen. The older the girl, the longer her dress. Young girls often wore pinafores over their dresses. Like aprons, these loose, sleeveless garments protected dresses from stains and spills. A girl pulled her pinafore on over her head and buttoned or tied it behind her neck.

A teacher *(next to stairs at left)* stands outside a school in Montana in the late 1800s, along with her students. The girls dressed as their mothers did, wearing calico dresses.

Many western pioneer families made yearly trips to town to buy supplies, including fabric, at a general store such as this one in Colorado.

READY-MADE

Western women didn't always have to make fabric and clothing from scratch. Most western towns had a general store, which sold household necessities. Everyday items included these:

- **fabric**
- **buttons**
- **thread**
- **needles**
- **ribbons**

General stores usually sold some ready-made clothing, such as denim blue jeans and overalls in standard sizes. Some stores even sold tailored men's

A group of dressmakers make clothing in 1890 in Minnesota with the help of the sewing machine. Their customers were probably wealthy women, the only ones who could afford to have clothing made to order.

suits and fancy women's gowns for special occasions. Many general stores employed part-time seamstresses or tailors, who made garments to order. Generally, only wealthy people could afford such custom-made clothing.

Large western cities, such as San Francisco and Sacramento, had some women's clothing stores, some of them owned and operated by women. The shops sold these ready-made clothes:

- **dresses**
- **hats**
- **undergarments**

The shops also employed seamstresses to make custom-made clothing for well-to-do women.

Fancy outfits such as this one were mostly worn by well-to-do women and girls. The young girl in this photograph has donned her finest clothing for a portrait. The outfit includes a formal dress, a straw hat, and tall boots with buttons.

MAIL-ORDER
FASHIONS

By the end of the 1800s, railroads crossed the American West, carrying both people and goods. The U.S. Post Office delivered mail and packages to many western cities. Even people who lived on remote farms could order goods by mail and pick them up in town. To feed the mail-order market, Sears, Roebuck and Company and Montgomery Ward mailed catalogs to potential customers throughout the United States. The 1897 Sears catalog assured westerners: "Don't think you live too far away. There is not a town in the United States where we have not sold goods."

With mail order, western women could purchase fashionable but affordable dresses, blouses, skirts, and jackets, in the same styles worn on the East Coast and even in Europe. For $4.85 a woman could purchase "the Exact Copy of a Parisian Cape." For $18 she could buy a fine suit, with a silk-lined cape, elaborately embroidered collar and lapels and a taffeta-lined, velvet-trimmed skirt. According to the catalog, the suit was "absolutely perfection in every respect."

Western buyers could thumb through mail-order catalogs such as this one to see and purchase the latest styles worn on the East Coast.

Showman William F. Cody, called Buffalo Bill, dressed like many fur traders and frontiersmen of the late 1800s. Here he wears a deerskin jacket with fringe and fur, along with animal skin pants and boots.

Chapter Three

RUGGED CLOTHING FOR RUGGED MEN

Some of the first white men in the American West were fur traders. At first, traders made business deals with Native Americans. The Indians trapped and killed animals and brought their furs to the white men's trading posts. In exchange for furs, white traders gave the Indians knives, guns, sugar, beads, cloth, and other manufactured items. Later, in the 1800s, many white men worked as fur trappers. They, too, brought their furs to sell at trading posts. Traders sold most of the furs they acquired to European merchants, who made them into clothing and hats. Beaver fur hats were particularly popular in Europe. Trappers also caught foxes, minks, rabbits, and other fur-bearing animals.

TRAPPER STYLE

Living on the frontier, fur trappers wanted clothing that was durable and practical. Native American–style clothing—shirts, pants, and

GOING, GOING, GONE

Because of the great demand for beaver fur in Europe for hats *(below)*, American trappers killed beavers by the hundreds of thousands. By the end of the 1800s, beavers were nearly extinct in North America.

Buffalo were also hunted almost to extinction. White hunters shot buffalo for sport and for their meat and hides. This hunting hurt Native Americans even further. Without buffalo for food, tools, and clothing, Indians could not survive.

moccasins made from the skins of buffalo and deer—fit the bill. Such clothing was strong, waterproof, and easy to patch. And the skins were easy to get. Hundreds of thousands of deer and buffalo roamed the American West.

For extra warmth in winter, trappers wore vests, boots, and mittens made from the skins of buffalo and deer. Trappers also wore some store-bought items, including cotton and woolen shirts and trousers. Some wore woolen coats, which doubled as warm blankets if they needed

to sleep outdoors. Buffalo skin robes were also extremely warm.

Osborne Russell, a trapper of the mid-1800s, kept a journal of his experiences out west. He described the clothing worn by his fellow trappers:

> His personal dress is a flannel or cotton shirt (if he is fortunate enough to obtain one, if not Antelope skin answers the purpose of over and under shirt) a pair of leather breeches [knee-length pants] with Blanket or smoked Buffaloe skin, leggings, a coat made of Blanket or Buffaloe robe a hat or Cap of wool, Buffaloe or Otter skin his hose are pieces of Blanket lapped round his feet which are covered with a

pair of Moccassins made of Dressed Deer Elk or Buffaloe skins with his long hair falling loosely over his shoulders complets his uniform.

Frontiersmen such as Kit Carson often dressed like Native Americans. They wore buckskin shirts, leggings, and moccasins.

"**ANY MAN WHO** WAS OUT IN THE OPEN IN WINTER WOULD HAVE ONE OF THESE WARM [BUFFALO] OVERCOATS."

—IDA ELLEN RATH, WRITING ABOUT WESTERN BUFFALO HUNTERS, 1961

While they frequently wore animal skins, white trappers didn't wear much animal fur themselves. The fur was too valuable. The men preferred to sell it for a nice profit.

LET'S BE PRACTICAL

Following the fur trappers and traders, more men came west in wagon trains, sometimes with their families and sometimes alone. Like female travelers, men wore sturdy, warm, and practical clothing on the westward journey. When these clothes became threadbare, some men dressed in deerskins. Others purchased new clothing from general stores or wore homespun outfits made by their wives.

Typical attire for a western farmer included these items:

- **a cotton or woolen shirt**
- **a vest**
- **trousers**

Men held up their pants with belts or suspenders. A jacket called a wamus or a roundabout completed the outfit. "This was a short jacket gathered into a belt at the bottom and finished at the neck with a close fitting straight or turn-over collar," explained Etta May Lacey Crowder. "The sleeves were gathered into a cuff which buttoned tightly around the wrist."

Overalls were popular with farmers and other men who worked outdoors. Some pairs were homemade out of coarse fabric or even grain sacks. For those who could afford better quality, Oregon City Woolen Mills made popular Hercules overalls, which sold for twelve dollars in 1868.

For special occasions, such as church services, western men wore white cotton dress shirts, woolen suit coats, and woolen trousers. Boys dressed like their fathers in these clothes:

- **cotton shirts**
- **overalls**
- **trousers**
- **suspenders**

The men on the right of this photo of a Nebraska farm family in 1885 are wearing sturdy, dark-colored work clothes. The man on the left side, however, is wearing a more formal white shirt. The woman on the right is also dressed in a more formal dress, while her female relative on the left wears a practical apron over a simple everyday dress.

RIDE 'EM COWBOY

If you lived in Texas from about 1865 to 1885, you were likely to run into some cowboys. These men drove cattle north along the Shawnee, Chisholm, the Goodnight-Loving, and other cattle trails. At railroad towns such as Abilene and Dodge City, Kansas, the cattle were loaded onto railcars, which carried them to slaughterhouses in Chicago, Illinois.

A cowboy's clothing needed to be durable because he spent most of his time outdoors, mainly on the back of a horse. A tall hat with a wide brim shielded his face from the harsh sun as well as the pouring rain. A long-sleeved shirt and long pants protected him from dust, wind, sunburn, and tumbles off his horse. Some cowboys liked wool pants, because they were warm and soft. Others preferred coarse

This cowboy is wearing fur-covered chaps—sometimes called woolies—along with his cowboy shirt, bandanna, and wide-brimmed hat.

A cowboy in Wyoming in the late 1800s is wearing typical cowboy gear—wide-brimmed hat, boots, fur-covered chaps, shirt, vest, and bandanna.

denim jeans. Still others wore deerskin pants like Native Americans. A leather vest gave the cowboy an extra layer of warmth. Most vests had pockets for holding tobacco, cigarette papers, watches, and other gear. In winter many cowboys wore buffalo robes.

Cowboys wore leggings called chaps over their pants. Chaps are made of two long, rectangular pieces of leather, which wrap around the legs and attach to each leg with a belt at the waist. Chaps protected cowboys from rope burns, falls, and horse bites. In heavy wind, rain, or snow, chaps helped keep cowboys' legs warm. On the northern plains in winter, some cowboys wore fur-covered chaps called woolies, or grizzlies.

Many cowboys wore brightly colored cotton bandannas around their necks. Blue and red were the most popular colors. A bandanna kept a cowboy's neck from getting sunburned or windburned. He could use the bandanna as a rag, a towel, or even a bandage. Some cowboys called them wipes, or wild rags.

SOLDIERS IN UNIFORM

Following the Civil War (1861–1865), the U.S. Army sent thousands of soldiers west—to the Great Plains and into the Southwest and the Rocky Mountains. From bases throughout the West, U.S. Army cavalrymen, or soldiers on horseback, patrolled the frontier, protected white travelers on overland trails, and battled with Indians. Enlisted, or rank-and-file, cavalrymen wore woolen or cotton shirts and trousers, blue woolen coats, and leather boots. Officers dressed in blue woolen greatcoats with these accessories:

- **capes**
- **brass buttons**
- **braiding**

Embroidered markings on their coats and hats showed their status as officers.

BUFFALO SOLDIERS

One group of western cavalrymen stood out from the others. They were African American soldiers who served in separate regiments from their white counterparts. Indians called these men buffalo soldiers, probably because their dark curly hair resembled the hair on the back of a buffalo. The black soldiers wore this name with pride. They dressed just like the other cavalrymen on the frontier, except the markings on their uniforms indicated that they were part of the all-black Ninth Regiment or Tenth Regiment of the U.S. Army. Only the officers in these units were white.

These soldiers from the 25th Infantry were stationed in Montana in 1890. Native Americans called the African American regiments buffalo soldiers.

RAILROAD MEN

In the 1860s, the U.S. government made a big push to connect the entire nation—from coast to coast—by rail. The government authorized two companies to lay tracks across the West. The Union Pacific Railroad worked westward, starting near Omaha, Nebraska. The Central Pacific Railroad worked eastward, starting from Sacramento, California. After more than six years, the two railroad lines met up in Promontory, Utah, on May 10, 1869.

The job of laying tracks across the West was enormous. It required blasting through two mountain chains: the Rockies and the Sierra Nevada. Both railroads needed thousands of laborers to get the job done. The Union Pacific hired many Irish and other European immigrants, as well as native-born Americans, to work on its section of track. The Central Pacific Railroad hired thousands of Chinese immigrants, in addition to men of other backgrounds.

Many of the Chinese railroad workers dressed just as they had in their home country. They wore these clothes:

- **shallow cone-shaped straw hats**
- **long cotton tunics**
- **loose trousers**
- **cloth shoes**

Some wore their hair in long braided pigtails. But in this era, it was not easy to be an immigrant in the United States. White, Euro-American railroad workers often ridiculed and harassed the Chinese laborers. To better fit in on the job, some Chinese workers cut their long hair and adopted the dress of their white colleagues: tough woolen shirts and trousers, with leather boots to protect their legs and feet.

These men worked for the Union Pacific Railroad in the 1860s laying railroad tracks across the western United States. The Chinese worker in the center wears a straw hat and a loose cotton tunic, while his African American and white coworkers wear brimmed hats and tucked-in shirts.

CLEANING *Up Their* ACT

Whether they came as soldiers, cowboys, miners, or railroad workers, most of the men who moved west in the 1800s were single. Women of this era were expected to marry, have children, and settle near their parents and childhood homes. They were certainly not supposed to head out west in search of riches—although a few did. As a result of such attitudes, men far outnumbered women in the American West. Luzena Stanley Wilson recalled attending a dance in Nevada City, California, with "twelve ladies present and about three hundred men."

Without many women to impress, many western men let themselves get grubby. A dance like the one in Nevada City offered men a rare opportunity to clean up and wear their best attire. "At that time it was the prevailing fashion for the gentlemen to attend social gatherings in blue woolen shirts, and with trousers stuffed into boot-tops," Wilson recalled.

CITY SLICKERS

Eventually the West became more settled. As towns grew, they needed doctors, bankers, lawyers, and office clerks. Instead of homespun shirts and trousers, these men wore styles similar to those worn on the East Coast at the same time. They wore white dress shirts under formal suits and vests. Some dress shirts even had ruffles and pleats. Men in offices wore neckties in various styles. Some were intricately knotted or wrapped around the neck several times. Others were droopy bowties.

If a man struck it rich in the goldfields or in business, he might flaunt his wealth with fine clothing and expensive jewelry. Newly rich men—and those who were already rich before they came west—followed the latest fashions coming out of Europe. They wore suits made of fine European wool, brocaded vests, and silk ties and shirts.

A gentleman wears a top hat, a shirt, a tie, a frock coat, trousers, and boots in this photo from 1860. Many city dwellers in the American West wore clothes similar in style to those worn on the East Coast during this era.

Chapter Four

COMPLETING HER OUTFIT

For western women, a calico dress was only the beginning. Women needed hats, hairdos, accessories, footwear, and underwear to complete their ensembles. Such extras varied greatly—depending upon whether one was a farmwife, a schoolteacher, or a society woman.

NO FUSS

Women on the frontier generally wore neat and simple hairstyles. The typical farm woman had many chores to do and didn't want to fuss with her hair. She needed it out of her eyes and off her face while she worked. So a farm woman usually braided her hair and pinned it on top of her head or tied it up in a bun. She secured it with barrettes or hairpins. Some women applied a little hair oil to hold their hair in place.

This woman poses for a portrait in 1880. She is wearing her best clothing, including a fancy hat with a flower, a dress with decorative velvet trim, and gloves.

This portrait of a woman in the late 1800s shows the simple hairstyle many women in the American West wore. It is pulled up on top of her head in a bun, with just a few wispy strands around her face.

Girls on the frontier displayed a little more flair with their hair. They often wore it long and loose around their shoulders. Some wore long braids. Others tied back their hair with bows and ribbons. Some girls and young women wore their hair in long ringlets.

Elaborate Updos

Women in western cities paid much more attention to their hair. They looked through fashion magazines, noting illustrations of the latest styles from the East. Some city women teased their long hair to make it look fuller before pinning it on top of their heads. Others wore earlocks, or curled locks of hair that fell in front of each ear. In the 1850s, a popular style was to part the hair in the middle and pull it back into a loose bun or braid. The hair on the sides of the head was then curled or teased into a frizz and left to fall loose over the ears. Bangs, also called fringe, came into style in about 1870.

Western women often decorated their hair with these accessories:

- **flowers**
- **jewelry**
- **ribbons**

Some wealthy women of the Southwest, like their Spanish ancestors, wore *peinetas* (combs) in their hair. These were made of tortoiseshell, gold, ivory, or silver.

This girl's hairstyle—ringlets tied back with a pretty bow—was a common look for young women in the 1800s.

For special events, western women in cities wore elegant gowns, carefully styled hair with lace and ribbons or bows, and decorative features such as jewelry and a fan.

Some western women wore hairpieces—sometimes made of human hair and sometimes of animal hair—for extra fullness. Secured with pins, hairpiece styles included:

- **braids**
- **curls**
- **ringlets**

They gave the illusion that the wearer had more hair or longer hair than she really did.

> **AFTER WASHING** THE HAIR SHOULD BE IMMEDIATELY **DRIED...** BRUSHED CONSTANTLY **IN THE SUN** OR BEFORE THE FIRE UNTIL ITS LIGHTNESS **AND ELASTICITY ARE FULLY RESTORED.**
>
> —*PETERSON'S MAGAZINE,* OFFERING ADVICE ON WOMEN'S HAIR CARE, SEPTEMBER 1864

AT THE DROP OF A HAT

Hats were an essential accessory for every western woman. In fact, in the 1800s, a woman was not considered properly dressed if she left her home without a hat. The prairie bonnet, or sunbonnet, was the most common hat for farm women. Made of gingham or calico, this hat had a large front brim to keep the sun out of the wearer's eyes. The hat also had a spacious cap to cover her hair in back. The bonnet tied beneath her chin. Many farm women wore day caps indoors. These simple cloth caps covered the back of the head and also tied beneath the chin.

In towns and cities, women could buy fancier hats from millinery (hatmaker) shops and general stores. Some of these headpieces were elaborate creations with these features:

- **broad brims**
- **masses of feathers**
- **ribbons**

The dress cap was a piece of dainty, decorative cloth, simply pinned to the hair in back of the head. In the Southwest, Spanish American women sometimes wore lacy head coverings called mantillas.

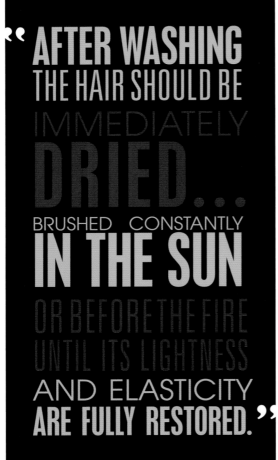

Sunbonnets, such as the one shown here, were popular and necessary for women in the American West in the 1800s. Women did much of their work outdoors, and the hats kept the sun from burning their skin.

SHOE LEATHER

I n the late 1800s, a pair of new shoes cost three to ten dollars. This was very expensive at the time, putting shoes out of reach for many farm families. To save on shoe leather, many westerners went barefoot at home and wore shoes only on special occasions. Sometimes a woman walked barefoot on short outings, such as a visit to a neighbor's home. She carried her shoes and stockings with her and put them on when she arrived. During warm weather, many children went barefoot to school. When parents did splurge on a pair of shoes for a child, they typically bought shoes that were too large. This way, the child could grow into the shoes and wear them for years.

For working outdoors and in cold weather, shoes were a necessity. Most western women wore sturdy, low-heeled, lace-up shoes and boots *(right)*. Some shoes had button closures. The wearer used a tool called a buttonhook to fasten and unfasten her shoes. High-heeled, ankle-high boots with pointy toes came into style in the 1870s.

ORNAMENTS AND
ACCESSORIES

Most frontier women wore little jewelry. A farmwife might wear just a wedding ring from day to day. She wore her other jewelry only on special occasions. Lockets were popular in the 1800s. These were small metal cases, worn on a chain around the neck. Western women put mementos, such as portraits or photos of loved ones, inside their lockets. Many women placed a lock of a sweetheart's hair inside a locket—especially if he had gone off to war. If the sweetheart died in battle, she might transfer the hair into a black mourning locket. Some western women wore small hook earrings. As was usually the case, wealthy townswomen wore more jewelry than working women on the frontier.

Many women in the American West wore lockets. The lockets usually held photos, a lock of hair, or another reminder of a loved one.

This illustration from *Godey's Lady's Book* features a woman holding a parasol (umbrella) and a reticule (handbag). *Godey's Lady's Book* was a popular fashion magazine of the 1800s.

Shawls in many fabrics and styles were popular for women in the 1800s. In this photo from 1862, Elizabeth Custer, wife of famous U.S. general George Armstrong Custer, wears a plaid shawl.

Wealthy women also had more accessories than poor women. These items included small, ornate handbags, which women carried inside pockets in their dresses or even in the folds of their dresses. Women also tucked handkerchiefs into their pockets or purses. Well-to-do women often carried parasols. These cloth umbrellas were frilly and stylish—but they were also practical. They protected a woman's skin from the harsh rays of the sun. Many women wore woolen shawls, both for beauty and warmth. Some shawls were decorated with beading or fringe. Many were hand knitted or crocheted.

Rich or poor, western women usually wore gloves. Wealthy women wore short, kid gloves during the daytime. These were made from kid, the soft skin of young goats. At night for formal dinners and social events, women wore long gloves made of satin or lace. Farming women usually wore plain cotton, wool, or animal skin gloves.

TIGHT CORSETS

The ideal of womanly beauty at this time was the hourglass figure—a full bust and hips and an extremely small waist. To reach this ideal shape, most women of the era wore corsets. These tight, vestlike garments were stiffened with thin strips of whalebone (which wasn't actually bone but came from the jaws of whales). Corsets fastened, either in front or back, with laces, clasps, or buttons. The tight garments constricted a woman's internal organs and made it difficult to move and even breathe.

Corsets weren't practical for every woman, especially not hardworking western women, who needed to bend and move freely to do a hard day's work. But women of this era were hesitant to defy convention. They didn't consider themselves properly dressed without corsets. Some western farm women loosened their corset strings when they worked. Others wore corsets only on the weekends. But they always wore them to social events and to church.

Women in the 1800s wore corsets such as the one shown here. The corsets were fastened tightly to give women an extremely small waist while accentuating their bust and hips.

THE LAYERED LOOK

The corset was just one of many layers worn beneath clothing by Victorian women—in the East and the West. Under her corset, a woman wore a chemise, also called a shift, or shimmy. It was a sleeveless, low-cut slip made of cotton or linen. Lightweight and easy to wash, the chemise absorbed sweat and also made a corset more comfortable. Many women wore a modesty piece on top of their corsets. This was a short collared top that covered a woman's neckline above her dress.

Some women wore a single petticoat, or underskirt, below their corsets. Others wore several petticoats. Layers and layers of petticoats helped fill out the space beneath

UNDER COVER

Although all western women wore underpants, it was considered improper to talk about them. Instead of "underpants," people spoke of wearing "drawers" or "linen" (underpants were typically made of linen). Women's underpants were fairly loose, with a hem that fell at the knee or just above the knee. Underpants often had ruffles.

a woman's skirt, further accentuating the appearance of big hips and a tiny waist. In cold weather, multiple petticoats also helped a woman stay warm.

Hoops and Bustles

The underclothing didn't end there. Like their sisters on the East Coast, women of the West, starting in the 1860s, wore hoop crinolines under their dresses and skirts. Crinolines were domelike frames made of metal hoops held together with bands of cloth. By making a skirt wider, crinolines made a woman's waist look smaller.

In the 1870s, the bustle replaced the hoop crinoline. The bustle was a cushion or pad that a women tied around her waist, behind her rear end and underneath her skirt. A bustle supported the heavy draping in the back of a dress. It kept the skirt from sagging or dragging on the ground, and it gave the desired full look in back.

American actress Ethel Wynne wears a dress with a bustle in the 1880s. Bustles were a type of undergarment that gave a full look to the back of a woman's dress.

This young woman was photographed in her metal hoops. The crinolines widened a woman's dress to further accentuate her waist.

Like corsets, hoops and bustles weren't comfortable or practical, and many western women chose not to wear them. For instance, schoolteachers had to move freely in the classroom and sit for hours. That couldn't be done with cumbersome equipment beneath a dress. But many western women did wear hoops and bustles. Some even added a western twist to the fashion. They abandoned manufactured hoops in favor of homemade hoops made from soft, bendable grape vines or willow tree branches.

GOING UP

In the West, the dress of a proper woman didn't always mesh with her rugged surroundings. In the 1800s, the West was dirty, dusty, and muddy. Even in towns, roads were unpaved. Piles of horse manure sat steaming in the streets.

When working outdoors, some farm women tied or rolled up their long skirts, so their hems wouldn't fray, rip, or get dirty. One entrepreneur gave western women another option. In Kansas the *Leavenworth Daily Times* ran an advertisement in December 1874. It offered an "instant dress elevator" for twenty-five cents. The device mechanically hiked up a woman's skirt to protect it from soiling. The advertisement boasted:

> You can raise your skirt while passing a muddy place and then let it fall, or you can keep it raised with the elevator. It keeps the skirt from filth. It can be changed from one dress to another in less than two minutes.

NIGHTY NIGHT

When the day was done, western women swapped their layers and layers of clothing for simple nightdresses. These floor- or ankle-length dresses were made of white cotton. They typically had high collars decorated with:

- **lace**
- **embroidery**
- **pleats**

The cuffs were similarly adorned. Upon going to bed and rising, some women wore short morning robes over their nightdresses. Most morning robes had a capelike design. They typically had loose sleeves and tied around the neck or at the waist.

Women also wore caps when they went to bed. A cap helped keep the wearer's head warm—especially important in drafty farmhouses. And because many women used hair oil to groom their hair, caps kept their pillows from getting greasy.

A woman braids her hair and reads a book before bed in this image from the late 1800s. She is wearing a typical nightdress of the era, made of white cotton.

Chapter Five

MANLY FLOURISHES

A western man's occupation influenced his choice of hairstyle. Men who roughed it in the wilderness, such as fur trappers, often let their hair grow long. Wild Bill Hickok, a western lawman and adventurer, wore his hair down to his shoulders. George Armstrong Custer, who died fighting Native Americans at the Battle of Little Bighorn in 1876, had a full head of curly long hair. Long hair on the frontier was partly a matter of practicality. Trappers' shacks, mining camps, and other western habitats had no running water. Water had to be hauled up from a well or carried from a nearby river, which made bathing and washing hair all the more trouble. In addition, far from cities, with few women around, many men felt no pressure to be clean or attractive.

In towns and cities, men could easily stop into a barbershop for a haircut and a shave. Many city dwellers wore their hair short and parted neatly down the middle or to one side. Like women, many men of this era treated their hair with oil, which kept it in place and made it slick and shiny.

Western lawman James Butler Hickok, also known as Wild Bill Hickok, was known for his long hair. In this photo, Hickok also sports a handlebar mustache, which was popular in the mid-1800s.

Whiskers

Facial hair was very common in this era. Some western men copied the style of Abraham Lincoln, the first U.S. president to wear a beard. Lincoln's distinctive look featured a short, groomed beard, accompanied by short hair and no mustache. The spade beard was another well-liked style out west. This was a bushy, short or medium-length beard with a point at the bottom, like the bottom tip of a shovel.

Mustaches were also common. The imperial mustache extended outward toward the ears, almost all the way across the face. Many men curled the edges of this mustache upward. The long, drooping handlebar mustache was popular in the 1870s and the 1880s. Wild Bill Hickok wore this style, along with his long hair.

Many western men grew sideburns. Originally called burnsides, sideburns were named for Northern Civil War general Ambrose Burnside, whose long bushy sideburns merged with his thick mustache. Another name for sideburns was muttonchops, because they resembled a piece of cut mutton, or lamb meat.

UNDER YOUR HAT

Whether he worked as a cowboy, a farmer, or a shopkeeper, a western man always wore a hat outside the house. The hat served to protect its wearer from rain, sun, snow, and wind, but it also gave him a dignified appearance. Like their female counterparts, men of the 1800s did not

Many western men didn't bother to shave at all. Some copied President Abraham Lincoln *(top)* and grew a beard but no mustache. Others copied Union (Northern) general Ambrose Burnside *(bottom)* and grew bushy sideburns.

Left: This man poses for a photo in the late 1800s wearing a wide-brimmed hat typical for outdoor wear in the West at that time.
Above: Men who worked indoors usually wore smaller-brimmed hats, such as the bowler pictured on western lawman and writer William Barclay (Bat) Masterson.

feel properly dressed without a hat. Hats of this era were usually made of these materials:

- **felt**
- **wool**
- **leather**
- **straw**

A hatband, made from leather, wool, braided horsehair, or ribbon, helped keep the hat securely on the wearer's head. Some hatbands were decorated with feathers or Indian beadwork.

ON THE JOB

Styles of hats varied, depending on where a man lived and the type of work he did. Farmers and others who labored outdoors preferred hats with wide brims, which protected their faces from the sun and rain. Men who worked indoors didn't need as much protection from the elements. They preferred bowlers and derbies. These were narrow-brimmed hats made of wool, felt, or animal hair. As part of their uniforms, soldiers with the U.S. Cavalry wore wide-brimmed felt hats with gold braided hatbands.

Cowboy hats were multipurpose tools. They protected a cowboy from sun and rain. But cowboys also used them to fan the flames of campfires and even to carry water. The Montana peak cowboy hat had a deep indentation in the crown, which helped drain rainwater from the top of the hat. The Southwest peak cowboy hat had several creases. Sombreros originated in Mexico. These cowboy hats had round crowns with no creases.

HOMEMADE HATS

Most men bought hats from a general store, a haberdasher (men's clothing store), or by mail. But some westerners made their own hats. Etta May Lacey Crowder's mother made straw hats for the men of her family. Crowder recalled:

Among the industries practiced at home . . . was the making of straw hats. Not everyone knew how to do this but mother was one who did. Before the first crops were raised, hats were made from blue joint, a wild grass which then grew rather tall on the uplands and had a stem very much like that of wheat. It was stiff and hard to work with and as soon as possible, wheat or oat straw was used. The straw was first plaited [braided], four or more strands together, then sewn into shape. The hats were fitted to the heads as they were

sewn, so the boys had to come into the house often and try them on. The hat was begun at the center of the crown, the braid sewed around and around until the required size was reached. Then it was turned by drawing the braid tighter and the crown was continued until the required height was reached. It was then turned again by sewing the braid more loosely and the brim was formed.

This westerner, photographed around 1890, wears a hat with a Montana peak, a deep indentation in the crown, which helped rain drain off the hat.

TO BOOT

Men who lived in town could purchase footwear at a general store or clothing shop. Starting in the 1870s, Montgomery Ward and Sears, Roebuck offered shoes through their mail-order catalogs. In addition, traveling shoemakers sometimes visited homes on the frontier. The shoemakers carried shoes in only a few sizes, which meant the customer wasn't always guaranteed a good fit. Some westerners made their own boots and moccasins out of deerskin. These were modeled after Native American footwear.

Buffalo hunters, miners, and other outdoorsmen usually wore ankle- or calf-high leather boots with square or rounded toes. These protected their legs and feet from thorns and snakebites. Cowboys also wore tall boots, but their boots had pointed toes. This shape was important, because sometimes cowboys needed to dismount their horses quickly. Their pointed boots would easily slip from their stirrups (metal frames that hung from a horse's saddle), whereas square-toed boots might get caught.

SPUR OF THE MOMENT

On the trail, cowboys wore metal spurs attached to their boots *(right)*. The spurs were both decorative and functional. Craftsmen made them in many styles. Spurs had short, sharp points. A cowboy used them to prod his horse and make it turn or run faster.

This cowboy was photographed in his wide-brimmed hat, fringed buckskin jacket, and calf-high leather boots. His boots also have spurs, which a cowboy could use to make his horse run faster.

Many men in the rugged West carried weapons. This American cowboy, for example, has a gun in a holster at his waist and a cartridge belt for ammunition. The man also holds a lasso, which cowboys used to rope horses and cattle.

GUNS AND AMMUNITION

In the Wild West, it was common to see men wearing pistols, which they kept inside holsters hung around their waists. In this vast, sparsely settled territory, lawmen were few and far between. Bandits and bank robbers frequently took what they pleased. So many ordinary men took the law into their own hands. They carried guns for self-defense and for fighting off any bad guys they encountered.

Soldiers and hunters always carried guns and rifles, along with cartridge belts to hold their bullets. Some hunters kept gunpowder in a powder horn, a container made of animal horn that was slung over one shoulder. Most western men also carried knives, used not only for self-defense but also for skinning animals and other tasks. Some men kept a knife tucked into the top of a boot.

Underalls

While women's underwear was complicated in the 1800s, men's undergarments were simple. Most men wore a union suit beneath their clothes. This was a one-piece garment with both long sleeves and long pant legs. Many trappers, buffalo hunters, and other western outdoorsmen wore leather breechcloths instead of cloth undergarments.

Men who lived in the wilderness didn't wear special sleepwear. They just slept in the clothes they wore in the daytime. Townsmen and farmers were more likely to change into nightshirts for sleeping. These were similar to women's nightdresses, only not as long. Many men also wore nightcaps to sleep.

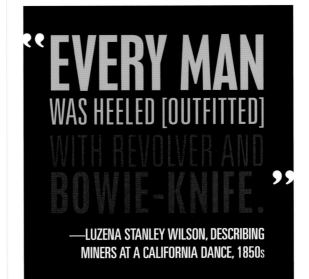

"EVERY MAN WAS HEELED [OUTFITTED] WITH REVOLVER AND BOWIE-KNIFE. **"**

—LUZENA STANLEY WILSON, DESCRIBING MINERS AT A CALIFORNIA DANCE, 1850s

ODDS AND ENDS

Western men donned a host of other accessories, depending on their jobs, tastes, and habits. Cowboys carried quirts and bullwhips, braided leather whips for lashing animals. Many outdoorsmen, such as hunters and trappers, kept their gear in leather knapsacks and carried water in leather pouches.

In the city, it was common to see men wearing pocket watches. These were stylish and functional pieces of jewelry. The watch fit conveniently in a vest pocket. It was secured to a buttonhole or belt loop with a long chain. Many western men smoked pipes, cigarettes, or cigars, which they also stored in their pockets.

CUFFS AND COLLARS

Many western men wore paper shirt collars and cuffs. These were stiff rings of paper, lined with linen, that attached to a shirt. When a collar or cuffs got dirty, a man simply threw them away and attached new ones. That way, he could always appear clean and sharply dressed, without having to constantly launder his shirts.

Some western styles were unique to a particular region or to the type of work a person did. For example, these Arizona cowboys wear chaps, work shirts, broad-brimmed hats, and weapons at the waist.

Chapter Six

TRENDSETTERS AND RULE BREAKERS

In most cases, westerners took their fashion cues from the East. They wore styles shown in fashion magazines. The ready-made clothing they purchased through mail-order catalogs was available to Americans nationwide. But many styles were unique to the West. Some, like buffalo robes and deerskin leggings, owed their origins to Native Americans. Others were created by western designers, specifically for western inhabitants.

PANTS FOR MINERS

In 1853, during the California gold rush, Levi Strauss, a young immigrant from Germany, moved to San Francisco. He planned to start a dry goods store, which would sell fabric, clothing, and small household articles. Strauss brought heavy canvas material with him on the trip west. He planned to make wagon covers and tents for gold miners with the canvas.

But the miners had something else in mind. Gold mining was rough work, they told Strauss when he reached the goldfields. Their flimsy cloth pants easily ripped and developed holes. The miners told Strauss that what they really needed were strong, sturdy trousers.

Strauss made the men trousers out of the canvas cloth he had brought with him. But the gold miners complained. The pants were too stiff and scratchy, they said. So Strauss tried another idea. He ordered a softer but still rugged, dark blue cloth from France. It was called serge de Nîmes, which eventually became known as denim.

When Levi Strauss came west in 1853, he learned that gold miners needed sturdy work clothing.

A few years later, Strauss acted upon the idea of a tailor named Jacob Davis, who suggested putting metal rivets along the seams of Strauss's jeans. The rivets made the pants extra strong. Strauss and Jacobs patented Levi's riveted blue jeans in 1873.

The California miners pictured here are wearing Levi Strauss's blue jeans, which have rivets at the seams.

MADE FOR COWBOYS

A Kansas shoemaker named Charles Hyer also designed clothing to suit the needs of westerners. His contribution was the cowboy boot, created in 1875. Hyer modeled the boot after those worn by soldiers during the Civil War. Hyer gave his boot a pointed toe, to keep it from getting caught in a cowboy's stirrups when he jumped—or was thrown—from his horse. Hyer's first cowboy boot was about 17 inches (43 centimeters) high—coming almost to the wearer's knee. Hyer sewed leather straps to the top of the boot at each side. The straps served as handles to help the wearer take his boots on and off.

John B. Stetson completed the cowboy's outfit with the creation of a tall, waterproof hat. Stetson was born in New Jersey in 1830. His family ran a haberdashery, a store that sold men's clothing and accessories. Stetson's father taught him the trade of hat making when he was a boy. In his twenties, he grew ill. A doctor suggested that he move west to get fresh air and improve his health.

In 1865 Stetson traveled through Colorado on his horse. There he designed a hat with a wide brim for protection from the rain. He gave the hat a waterproof lining and made it 6 inches (15 cm) deep, so he could use it to carry water for himself and his horse.

Stetson made a few extra copies of the hat. He hung them from his saddle. One day a cowboy saw the dangling hats and asked if he could buy one. After this first sale, Stetson returned east and began a business. With only one hundred dollars to his name, he bought ten dollars worth of fur and rented a small room in Philadelphia. He named his business the John B. Stetson Hat Company. At first he called his new product the Hat of the West. People later called his creation the Boss of the Plains or simply a Stetson.

John B. Stetson designed the most well-known cowboy hat of all. Each Stetson had a wide brim to keep sun off the wearer's face. One version of the hat, shown at right, had an extremely high crown. Some cowboys even used the hat to carry water.

PUSHING THE **LIMITS**

In this era, most American women dressed modestly. They rarely wore makeup. They covered their bodies from neck to ankle with layers and layers of clothing. For a woman to show even her bare arms was considered improper. Western women wanted to follow the rules. They wanted to be ladylike in dress and behavior. But restrictive corsets, crinolines, and layers of petticoats weren't well suited to the life of a western woman.

In New York, a woman named Elizabeth Smith Miller invented bloomers in 1850. Named for women's rights activist Amelia Bloomer, bloomers were baggy, calf-length trousers that women could wear beneath their skirts. The style didn't really catch on in the East, but it was perfect for women of the West. Dressed in bloomers, a western woman could ride a horse or tend a farm with ease and comfort. On the overland trail west, Jane Kellogg wore "bloomers all the way, the better to enable us to walk through the sagebrush. They were made with short skirts and pants reaching to the shoe tops. Everyone wore them."

But even in the rugged West, some people weren't quite ready for bloomers. "It's a disgrace to see a female dressed in trousers—an offense to the very fabric of civilization," wrote Arlo Howell, a Colorado miner in 1853. "I was witness to a display of 'bloomers' the other day. The young woman's skirt was unusually short. It was an outrage!"

Bloomers *(top left)* were named for women's rights activist Amelia Bloomer *(right).* Western women liked the style because it gave them freedom of movement.

SPREADING THE WORD

Westerners of the 1800s had only a few ways to keep up with fashion trends on the East Coast and Europe. The primary vehicle for this information was women's magazines such as *Godey's Lady's* Book, *Harper's Bazaar*, *Peterson's Magazine*, and the *Delineator*. These publications featured detailed fashion plates (such as the one shown below in *Peterson's* from 1877), or illustrations of women in stylish clothing. Some magazines included sketches of sewing patterns. A woman could copy the patterns to sew clothing for her own family. *Peterson's Magazine* offered a monthly feature called "New Styles of Wearing the Hair," which showed women with elaborate hairdos, often adorned with braids, ribbons, flowers, and curls. The magazines also carried advertisements for clothing patterns, baby clothes, jewelry, and fashion accessories.

Mail-order catalogs were another good source of fashion information. The catalogs featured drawings and descriptions of popular styles. The catalogs helped ensure that even on the isolated frontier, a westerner would never be too far out of vogue.

THE **SHOCK** FACTOR

Some western women took the shock and outrage to the next level. Female dancers and actresses broke all the rules when it came to dress and decorum. They put makeup on their faces and wore revealing costumes onstage. One performer, Lola Montez, dazzled gold miners with her sexy dancing. Another, Adah Menken, caused a major stir in the summer of 1863 in San Francisco. There, she starred in a play called *Mazeppa*. In one scene, she shocked the cultured and elegantly dressed theatergoers by appearing onstage, on horseback, in nothing but a light-colored body stocking. Menken's revealing outfit was the talk of the town for weeks after her performance. Offstage, Menken was just as daring. She wore typical men's clothing instead of women's.

SALOON GIRLS AND *Fancy Ladies*

More rule breakers worked in western saloons, hangouts for rowdy miners, gamblers, and cowboys. The "saloon girls" or "fancy ladies" who worked there did more than serve drinks and food. They usually also worked as prostitutes. With men greatly outnumbering women in the West, these women did a steady business.

Saloon girls certainly didn't dress like prim farmwives or schoolteachers. They wore brightly colored gowns, dresses, and stockings. They styled their hair in elaborate updos. Many wore heavily applied makeup, which earned them the nickname painted ladies. One observer noted western prostitutes with "chalk white faces" and "scarlet painted lips and cheeks."

Revealing clothing was strictly forbidden for women in the West. Occasionally, however, women broke the rules. Actress Adah Menken, shown here in 1862, was known for her exotic and daring costumes.

A WOMAN CALLED
CALAMITY

Like Adah Menken, Martha Canary also dressed like a man. And she wore her hair long and dirty. Canary was born in 1852 near Princeton, Missouri. Her family moved west in 1865. Young Martha didn't behave like other girls. At thirteen she learned to tame and ride wild horses. Her brothers and father taught her to hunt.

By 1870 Canary was a skilled sharpshooter, meaning she had perfect aim with a gun. She was also an excellent rider. Her skills earned her a job with George Armstrong Custer of the U.S. Army. She worked as a scout—someone who moves ahead of the main unit of soldiers, looking out for the enemy. At this point, Canary stopped wearing women's clothing and started dressing like a soldier.

According to one story, Canary earned her nickname after an Indian attack on her unit. Her commander, Captain Egan, was injured in the attack, and she carried him to safety on her horse. When Egan recovered from his injuries, he said to Canary, "I name you Calamity Jane, the heroine of the plains."

Calamity Jane threw out all the rules for respectable women of the West by wearing buckskin clothing and scouting for the U.S. Army.

> "UP TO THIS TIME I HAD ALWAYS WORN THE COSTUME OF MY SEX. WHEN I JOINED [LIEUTENANT COLONEL GEORGE] CUSTER I DONNED THE UNIFORM OF A SOLDIER. IT WAS A BIT AWKWARD AT FIRST BUT I SOON GOT TO BE PERFECTLY AT HOME IN MEN'S CLOTHES."
>
> —MARTHA "CALAMITY JANE" CANARY, FRONTIERSWOMAN, 1870s

Calamity Jane was certainly out of the ordinary for women of her era. But she wasn't completely alone. Many western women did rough, dirty jobs that were normally held by men. They worked as cowgirls, ranchers, and farmers. They showed that women could be as tough and determined as any man.

Wilde Man

When Irish author and playwright Oscar Wilde visited the West in the 1880s, he also made quite a stir. Wilde was a part of the European aesthetic movement. This group of artists and freethinkers emphasized beauty in art, design, and literature. Aesthetics opposed the restrictive, often uncomfortable clothing worn at the time. They preferred loosely cut garments made of natural, soft fabrics such as:

- **silk**
- **velvet**
- **satin**

In the early 1880s, Wilde traveled across the United States on a lecture tour. He visited western towns, including Leadville, Colorado, and San Francisco. Afterward, reporters commented at length about his clothing, particularly his velvet suit, frilly shirts, knee-length pants, flowing tie, and knee-high boots. Wilde showed that men, like women, could wear beautiful, luxurious clothing. Even so, most western men stuck with their more tightly tailored attire.

Oscar Wilde is photographed here in the late 1800s. His clothing, made from luxurious, soft fabrics, was much less rugged than what men in the American West were wearing at the time.

This family farmed in Arizona in the 1800s. Clothing styles in the American West, especially on farms and on the frontier, remained simple and practical even as fashions changed rapidly in the East.

EPILOGUE

With the beginning of a new century in 1900, Americans could see newness everywhere, especially in big cities. Electric trolleys rolled down city streets. Automobiles, almost unknown just ten years earlier, were becoming common. Some people had telephones in their homes. Some homes had electric lights and running water. The world was changing.

SLOWER OUT WEST

The American West was changing too—but not quite as fast. The new inventions were slow to reach the frontier. Most westerners continued to farm the land just as their parents and grandparents had done. They still hauled water in buckets from wells. They still read and mended clothing by the light of kerosene lanterns at night. Cowboys and ranchers still tended their animals on horseback.

Because western life was just as gritty and rugged as ever, western clothing needed to remain gritty and rugged as well. The styles developed during earlier decades, especially for men, changed very little. Cowboys still wore chaps and Stetson hats. Miners and other laborers still wore Levi's blue jeans. Farmers still wore overalls. This clothing was sturdy and long lasting. People saw no need to change it.

American movie star Louise Brooks became famous for her bobbed hairstyle in the 1920s. As more Americans went to the movies, they modeled their styles on what they saw actors and actresses wearing in films.

TIME MARCHES ON

Women's fashions did change, however. On the East Coast, women began wearing shorter skirts and dresses. The change was incremental—just a few inches at first. But before long, women were in the middle of a full-blown fashion revolution. Starting in the 1910s, skirts got shorter and shorter until they finally rested at the wearer's knee. Women started showing bare arms and low necklines. Women then cast off their corsets in favor of lightweight slips and bras. Women's hairstyles changed too. Bobbed hair—a short boyish cut—came into vogue. And more and more women began wearing makeup. "Face paint" was no longer scandalous—the sign of a wicked, painted lady. Instead, it was a sign of high fashion.

When styles changed in the East, they changed in the West too. Western women were a bit more conservative than their eastern sisters. They didn't embrace new styles quite so quickly. But there was no holding back progress. By the 1920s, petticoats and corsets were practically museum pieces. Cowgirls and other western women began to bob their hair and shorten their skirts. Also following eastern trends, men of the West cut their hair short and shaved off their big beards and side whiskers. Vests, bowties, pocket watches, and button shoes all fell by the wayside. The Old West was gone—or was it?

Myth Making

Around this time, the movie business hit its stride. From their studios in Hollywood, California, filmmakers explored every genre: science fiction, romance, slapstick, swashbucklers, and westerns, which were always a box office favorite. Up on the silver screen, the Old West looked romantic and exciting. Filmmakers played up all sorts of stereotypes. Characters included:

- **virtuous frontier women**
- **daring cowboys**
- **valiant cavalry troopers**
- **sassy saloon hall girls**
- **Indians in feathered headdresses**

Advertisers too used images of the Wild West to sell everything from cigars to soap.

As the twentieth century moved on, the West continued to change. Farms became mechanized. Western homes got electric power. Western cities got bigger, with more and more cars and industry. But in the public imagination, the West remained frozen in time. Easterners took western vacations to experience the allure of the Old West. They visited dude ranches (western-themed resorts) in Arizona, ghost towns in Colorado, and old silver mines in Nevada. At roadside gift shops, they bought these items:

- **sombreros**
- **moccasins**
- **fringed deerskin dresses**

Cowboy movies such as *In Old Oklahoma* (1943), starring John Wayne, painted a romantic image of the Old West. The films inspired many boys to dress like cowboys.

On the East Coast, little boys dressed like cowboys and Indians for Halloween. Television got into the act, with show after show about cattle ranchers, Indian fighters, and pioneers.

In the twenty-first century, the Old West hasn't lost its allure. If anything, western fashion is more popular than ever. Those Levi's jeans that first went on sale in the 1850s are a staple in every mall in every city in the United States. In the twenty-first century, you're just as likely to see cowboy boots in New York City as in San Antonio, Texas. Some parts of the Old West—gunslingers, saloon hall girls, and buffalo hunters—might be gone forever. But in the world of fashion, the American West lives on.

Western fashions haven't lost their appeal. These modern teenagers in the United States both wear Western-influenced clothes. The boy wears a denim jacket, jeans, and a cowboy hat. The girl wears cowboy boots.

TIMELINE

LATE **1500**s
Spanish settlers introduce sheep to Navajo people in the American Southwest. The Navajo begin to raise their own sheep and use the wool to make clothing.

1850
Elizabeth Smith Miller invents bloomers, women's knee-length trousers worn under a short skirt. The pants are named for Amelia Bloomer, a women's rights activist who helped make them popular.

1853
In San Francisco, merchant Levi Strauss begins making sturdy denim jeans for gold miners.

1860s
Thousands of Chinese immigrants help build the transcontinental railroad. Many dress in Chinese-style clothing, including cone-shaped straw hats, long tunics, loose trousers, and cloth shoes.

1863
Actress Adah Menken shocks audiences in San Francisco by appearing onstage in only a light-colored body stocking.

1865–1885
Cowboys drive cattle north from Texas to railroad towns in the Midwest. Their accessories include tall hats, leather chaps, tall boots, spurs, and bandannas.

1870
In Wyoming, Martha "Calamity Jane" Cannary becomes a scout for George Armstrong Custer of the U.S. Army. Cannary wears trousers, a leather jacket, tall boots, and other clothing typically worn by male soldiers.

1873
Levi Strauss patents his riveted blue jeans. The jeans have metal rivets, which strengthen the seams.

1873–1882
British writer Oscar Wilde gives a series of lectures in the United States, including in several western towns. Audiences take note of his velvet suit, frilly shirts, and other luxurious clothing.

1874
The *Leavenworth (KS) Daily Times* advertises an "instant dress elevator," a device for hiking up women's skirts to protect them from mud and dirt.

1875
Shoemaker Charles Hyer designs a boot specifically for cowboys, with a pointed toe and leather straps at the top. Hatmaker John B. Stetson designs a tall, wide-brimmed, waterproof cowboy hat.

1880s
Boarding schools for Native Americans open in western states. The schools dress students in European-style clothing and cut their hair into styles worn by white Americans.

GLOSSARY

bandanna: a large, colorfully patterned handkerchief, frequently worn by cowboys in the American West

bodice: the upper portion of a woman's dress

breechcloth: a long strip of deerskin or another material worn between the legs, with front and back panels hanging down from a band at the waist. In the Old West, many Native American men and white frontiersmen wore breechcloths.

breeches: tight-fitting men's pants that reach to the knee

buckskin: a soft leather made from the hide of a male deer

bustle: a cushion or pad worn beneath the back of a dress or skirt to give it fullness

chaps: wide leather leggings joined together by a belt. Cowboys often wear chaps to protect their legs.

chemise: a sleeveless cotton or linen slip, usually worn under a corset in the 1800s

corset: a vestlike undergarment, stiffened with whalebone, worn by women in the 1800s. Corsets tightly constricted the waist to give the body an hourglass shape.

crinolines: a series of metal hoops worn beneath a skirt to give it fullness

fashion plate: a fashion illustration in a magazine of the 1800s

haberdasher: a merchant who sells men's clothing and accessories

hide: the skin of an animal, often used to make leggings, shirts, dresses, and other garments

kid gloves: gloves made from the skin of a young goat

leather: animal skin that has been treated with chemicals to keep it from decaying. Leather was used to make boots, hats, and other clothing in the American West.

locket: a small metal case for holding a memento, such as the lock of a loved one's hair. Lockets were typically worn on a chain around the neck.

mantilla: a lightweight scarf worn over the head and shoulders, often worn by Spanish American women in the Southwest

milliner: a person who makes or sells women's hats

moccasins: slipperlike leather shoes, first worn by Native Americans in many parts of North America. Moccasins were often decorated with beadwork.

overalls: a garment consisting of trousers, a bib above the waist, and shoulder straps

petticoat: an underskirt worn beneath a skirt or dress

ready-made clothing: clothing made in standard sizes for sale to the general public, not custom-made for a particular buyer

sombrero: a tall hat with a rounded, uncreased crown, often worn by cowboys in the American Southwest. The style came to the United States from Mexico.

spin: to twist raw wool, flax, or other fibers into yarn or thread

spur: a pointed metal device worn on a rider's boot, used for urging on a horse

whalebone: stiff material from plates in the jaws of certain whales, used to stiffen corsets in the 1800s

SOURCE NOTES

9   John Ball, "Autobiography of John Ball," Library of Western Fur Trade Historical Source Documents, n.d., http://mtmen.org/mtman/html/jball.html (February 23, 2011).

13 Zitkala-Sa, "Impressions of an Indian Childhood," *Atlantic Monthly* 85 (January 1900).

16 Luzena Stanley Wilson, "Luzena Stanley Wilson '49, Her Memoirs as Taken Down by her Daughter in 1881," *New Perspectives on the West*, 2001, http://www.pbs.org/weta/thewest/resources/archives/three/luzena.htm (August 10, 2010).

16 Etta May Lacey Crowder, "Memoirs," Celtic Cousins, 2001, http://www.celticcousins.netirishiniowa/pioneerclothing.htm (February 23, 2011).

17 Florence Courtney Melton, "History of a Pioneer Family," Rootsweb, February 11, 2002, http://freepages.genealogy.rootsweb.ancestry.com/~cchouk/courtney (August 3, 2010).

17 T. T. Geer, *Fifty Years in Oregon* (New York: Neale Publishing Company), n.p.

21 Sears, Roebuck & Co., *Sears Roebuck & Co. Catalogue* (Chicago: Sears, Roebuck & Co., 1897), 1.

21 Ibid., 291.

21 Ibid., 298.

23–24 Osborne Russell, "Diaries, Narratives, and Letters of the Mountain Men," Library of Western Fur Trade Historical Source Documents, n.d., http://www.xmission.com/~drudy/mtman/html/ruslintr.html (February 23, 2011).

24 Ida Ellen Rath, *The Rath Trail* (Wichita, KS: McCormick-Armstrong Co., 1961), 78.

25 Crowder, "Memoirs."

29 Wilson, "Luzena Stanley Wilson."

29 Ibid.

32 "Editor's Table," *Peterson's Magazine*, September 1864, n.p.

37 Dee Brown, ed., *The Gentle Tamers: Women of the Old Wild West* (Lincoln: University of Nebraska Press, 1958), 134.

41 Etta May Lacey Crowder, "Memoirs."

44 Wilson, "Luzena Stanley Wilson."

49 Lillian Schlissel, ed., *Women's Diaries of the Westward Journey* (New York: Schocken Books, 1982), 105.

49 Chris Enss, *How the West Was Worn* (Guilford, CT: TwoDot, 2006), 30.

51 Sara E. Quay, *Westward Expansion* (Westport, CT: Greenwood Press, 2002), 98.

52 Roberta Beed Sollid, *Calamity Jane: A Study in Historical Criticism*, (Helena: Western Press /Montana Historical Society Press 1958), 127.

52 Ibid., 126.

SELECTED BIBLIOGRAPHY

Brown, Dee, ed. *The Gentle Tamers: Women of the Old Wild West*. Lincoln: University of Nebraska Press, 1958.

Enss, Chris. *How the West Was Worn*, Guilford, CT: TwoDot, 2006.

Nelson, Lynn H. "The American West," Virtual Library: History, August 20, 2009, http://www.vlib.us/americanwest/ (February 23, 2011).

PBS. *New Perspectives on the West*. Public Broadcasting Service. 2011. http://www.pbs.org/weta/thewest/ (February 23, 2011).

Quay, Sara E. *Westward Expansion*. Westport, CT: Greenwood Press, 2002.

Salisbury, Joyce. *The Greenwood Encyclopedia of Daily Life*. Vol. 5, *19th Century*. Santa Barbara, CA: Greenwood Press, 2004.

Schlissel, Lillian, ed. *Women's Diaries of the Western Journey*, New York: Schocken Books, 1982.

FURTHER READING AND WEBSITES

BOOKS

George-Warren, Holly. *The Cowgirl Way: Hats Off to America's Women of the West*. New York: Houghton Mifflin Books for Children, 2010.
With dynamic photos and plentiful quotes, the author gives the history of cowgirls—from the Old West to modern times.

Krohn, Katherine. *Women of the Wild West*. Minneapolis: Twenty-First Century Books, 2006.
Learn about the remarkable women who helped settle the West, including Annie Oakley, Calamity Jane, and the Unsinkable Molly Brown.

Littlefield, Holly. *Children of the Indian Boarding Schools*. Minneapolis: Lerner Publications Company, 2001.
Between 1879 and the early 1900s, the U.S. government took thousands of Native American children from their homes and families to be educated in distant boarding schools. The students were forced to abandon their cultural traditions and act like European Americans. This book examines this difficult episode in Native American history.

Markel, Rita J. *Your Travel Guide to American's Old West*. Minneapolis: Twenty-First Century Books, 2004.
If you were a traveler in the Old West, what would your trip be like? What would you eat? What clothing would you wear? Who would you be likely to meet? This guidebook takes the modern reader on a visit to the Old West.

McPherson, Stephanie Sammartino. *Levi Strauss*. Minneapolis: Lerner Publications Company, 2007.
Levi Strauss made a fortune selling sturdy denim pants to gold miners in the American West. This book tells his story—and the story of the jeans that made him rich and famous.

Williams, Colleen. *What the Native Americans Wore.* Broomall, PA: Mason Crest Publishers, 2002. This book examines Native American clothing in great detail. Each chapter focuses on a different region and tells how people used local plants and animals to make practical and decorative clothing and accessories.

WEBSITES

Buns and Baskets
http://howtodresslikeapioneer.blogspot.com
This blog shows you how to make historically accurate pioneer clothing, including sunbonnets, suspenders, and pinafores. The blogger cites nineteenth-century sources such as *Godey's Lady's Book* and *The Workwoman's Guide*. She also reproduces archival photographs and illustrations of pioneer fashions.

How the West Was Worn
http://www.autrynationalcenter.org/pdfs/how_the_west_was_worn.pdf
This online activity guide, created by the Autry Museum of Western Heritage, provides snapshots of western wear from the 1800s to modern times.

Indian Tanning
http://mdc.mo.gov/discover-nature/how/historic-crafts-and-skills/leatherworking/indian-tanning
This Web page from the Missouri Department of Conservation shows you how to tan hides the Indian way. You can get all the materials you need, even animal brains, from butcher shops, grocery stores, and hardware stores.

National Cowboy and Western Heritage Museum
http://www.nationalcowboymuseum.org
The museum's website includes extensive information on cowboys and other westerners, with discussions of western fashion and cowboy clothing.

INDEX

ABOUT THE AUTHOR

Katherine Krohn is the author of many books for young readers, including *Women of the Wild West* and the biographies *Princess Diana* and *Ella Fitzgerald: First Lady of Song*. She loves movies, feels most at home by the ocean, and does all of her writing in a vintage Airstream trailer. She lives in Oregon with her husband, Sheggy; their dog, Lucky; and cats, Ursula, Missy, and Moon Pie.

PHOTO ACKNOWLEDGMENTS

The images in this book are used with the permission of: © Jameswimsel/Dreamstime.com, pp. 1, 58; Courtesy, Colorado Historical Society pp. 3, (93.322.1087), 32, (CHS-X3587); The Granger Collection, New York, pp. 4, 7 (bottom), 12, 13, 16 (bottom), 18 (both), 19 (top), 22, 24, 25, 26 (bottom), 30 (right), 36 (both), 37, 38, 40 (right), 44, 47 (bottom), © Roger Fenton/Hulton Archive/Getty Images, p. 5; The Denver Public Library, Western History Collection, Louis R. Bostwick, X-33939, p. 6; National Anthropological Archives, Smithsonian Institution, pp. 7 (top), (BAE GN 01262 06246900), 11 (BAE GN 07188A 06306500); Courtesy, National Museum of the American Indian, Smithsonian Institution pp. 8, (P13053), 9 (left), (P03410); © 2002-2009 Peabody Museum, Harvard University, pp. 9 (right), 995-29-10/73240, 10 (right), 11-60-10/84012; © Richard A. Cooke/CORBIS, p. 10 (left); Courtesy, Colorado Historical Society (98.273.39/ Eugenia Ransom Kennicott), p. 14; Courtesy, Colorado Historical Society (90.156.1156/Harry H. Buckwalter), p. 16 (top); Minnesota Historical Society, p. 17; The Denver Public Library, Western History Collection, X-11702, p. 19 (bottom); Fred Mueller, Minnesota Historical Society, p. 20 (top); © R v Green/Hulton Archive/Getty Images, p. 20 (bottom); © Chicago History Museum /Contributor/Getty Images, p. 21; Library of Congress pp. 23 (top), (LC-USZ62-91125), 31 (top), (LC-USZ62-136958), 39 (top), (LC-DIG-ppmsca-19305), 39 (bottom), (LC-DIG-cwpb-05368), 49 (top), (LC-USZC2-1978), 52, (LC-USZ62-95040), 53, (LC-USZ62-85837); © Robert Holmes/CORBIS, p. 23 (bottom); The Denver Public Library, Western History Collection, Charles D. Kirkland, X-21939, p. 26 (top); © Everett Collection/Alamy, p. 27; The Denver Public Library, Western History Collection, E. & H.T. Anthony (Firm), Z-3335, p. 28; © Hulton Archive/Stringer/Getty Images, p. 29, 51; © Buyenlarge/Getty Images, p. 30 (left); © Henry Guttmann/Stringer/Hulton Archive/Getty Images, p. 31 (bottom); © Steve Cole/Photodisc/Getty Images, p. 33 (top); © D. Hurst/Alamy, p. 33 (bottom); Courtesy Everett Collection, pp. 34 (left), 35; © Medford Historical Society Collection/CORBIS, p. 34 (right); Courtesy, Colorado Historical Society (93.322.3587/Oliver E. Aultman), p. 40 (left); The Denver Public Library, Western History Collection, Z-6082, p. 41; © Lennette Newell/Workbook Stock/Getty Images, p. 42; The Art Archive/Bill Manns, pp. 43, 46, 48 (right) © Dictionary of American Portraits, pp. 47 (top), 49 (bottom); © CORBIS, p. 48 (left); © Kean Collection/Archive Photos/Getty Images, p. 50; © A.J. Ross/FPG/Archive Photos/Getty Images, p. 54; © John Kobal Foundation/Hulton Archive/Getty Images, p. 55; In Old Oklahoma, (aka War of the Wildcats)/Everett Collection, p. 56; © Tony Anderson/Photographer's Choice/Getty Images, p. 57.

Front Cover: Courtesy, Colorado Historical Society/Oliver E. Aultman.
Back Cover: The Denver Public Library, Western History Collection, Kohlberg & Hopkins, X-31968.

Main body text provided by Mixage ITC Book 10/15
Typeface provided by International Typeface Corp